TO: John &

Wishing you happiness.

Love y'all,
Carole Deffes Kelly

God's grace is
breathtaking!

♡ xoxoxoxo

WORDS OF WISDOM
CALENDAR

CAROLE DEFFES KELLY

WESTBOW
PRESS®
A DIVISION OF THOMAS NELSON
& ZONDERVAN

Scripture quotations taken from the New American Standard Bible® (NASB), Copyright © 1960, 1962, 1963, 1968, 1971, 1972, 1973, 1975, 1977, 1995 by The Lockman Foundation. Used by permission. www.Lockman.org

WestBow Press books may be ordered through booksellers or by contacting:

WestBow Press
A Division of Thomas Nelson & Zondervan
1663 Liberty Drive
Bloomington, IN 47403
www.westbowpress.com
1 (866) 928-1240

ISBN: 978-1-9736-0249-1 (sc)
ISBN: 978-1-9736-0248-4 (e)

Library of Congress Control Number: 2017916475

Print information available on the last page.

WestBow Press rev. date: 10/23/2017

INTRODUCTION

This is a 366-day calendar written by Carole Deffes Kelly, a servant of God our Father, Lord, and Savior Jesus Christ. It consists of some things God wants us to know and live by daily. They are words of wisdom for everyday life. Each day is a saying followed by a scripture taken from God's Word. The Bible is God's message to all of us. Jesus is saying, "I love you." He created you and wants you to love him back. Religion and rituals are for people to feel good about themselves. More importantly, God wants an intimate relationship with you aside from church and rituals. Jesus is waiting for you. He tells you to come to him with your burdens, and he will give you rest and peace in your life.

God does incredible things if we let his power work through us. There is no peace or true enjoyment in life apart from him. He tells us in Ecclesiastes 3, "There is a time for everything under the sun. There's a time for birth, a time to die, a time to plant, a time to uproot, a time to weep, a time to laugh, a time to mourn, a time to dance, a time for war, a time for peace and so on."

God is like a breeze. You can feel a breeze and see the effect of it, but you can't actually see it. Draw close to him so you can feel his spirit of peace, love, and joy in your heart and soul for now and all eternity.

Many people don't understand the trinity: Father, Son, and the Holy Spirit. It's a mystery. Here is an attempt to explain the one true God that is the Trinity. God is one God with three roles. The father is the creator, mastermind, and author of the plan. The Son Jesus is the executor of God's plan in the flesh. The Holy Spirit is the power behind God's plan in the Spirit. God, the Father, is Jesus Christ and the Holy Spirit. He is the one true God of the Bible and our Savior.

John 1:14 says, "The word became flesh and dwelt among us." God came to earth in the flesh of Jesus. He had to be the human sacrifice in our place to pay for all sin. He did it for all of us because we were all born into sin and would never be able to get right with God.

Jesus's life was God's gift to mankind. He gave himself. It's a gift you can't earn or pay for. Thank God for his grace and mercy.

Jesus came from a perfect heaven to live among the people he created, and we killed him! Only because he allowed man to kill him so he could pay for our sins with his life. That's why he had to pick the exact time in history to enter the world for us.

Sin has to die. Adam and Eve rebelled against God in the garden and listened to Satan, who deceived them. From then on, sin kept breeding. Back in the days of Abraham and Moses, God required people to make animal sacrifices to cover their sins until the time was right for Jesus to come into the world to be the one and only sacrifice for all. Jesus, who is God, came to earth to sacrifice himself for us. The God of all creation bought us back from Satan.

We don't understand many things because he's God and we're not. We are his creation. We are nothing but dust without him.

In my life God has given, I lived without him for many years. Around the age of thirty-five, I gave my life to Christ Jesus. I'm at peace in my soul, even with lots of turmoil and opposition all around me. I still make plenty of mistakes, but when I fall, he picks me up, brushes me off, and sets me on my way again to have learned another lesson in my life. He is a loving, consistent God that shows no partiality to his children. He loves us all the same. I don't know how I lived all those years without him. It was, without a doubt, my loss at that time.

God has given us all a free will to choose. I've been on both sides of that fence. When you walk away from God, you slowly walk deeper into sin. Resistance to God is futile! When I asked Christ into my life, he made me whole again. He put his Holy Spirit in me, and I began to see things in a different way because he was living in me. It was like a light bulb came on and I could see things clearer.

He asks us to love others the way he loves us. We can't do that without him because of being born with a sinful nature. We only know how to love others out of our own selfish needs. We ask ourselves,

"What's in it for me?" God helps us not to think that way anymore. He teaches us to put others first. They are more important than I am.

I'm still a miracle in progress until the day he takes me home, where I came from.

Pray and ask God to help you love the people who are unlovable. They can make your life miserable, but remember, God loves them too. He can help you work through it. If you don't have God working through you, your dislike will turn into bitterness and hate.

God has given us a free will. We can accept or reject him. You are free to go in any direction you want, but there is no middle ground. If you don't accept him, you automatically reject him. He tells us that in his Word.

God loves you, and he's waiting for you to love him back. Don't miss out on the richest blessing in your life.

Jesus tells us in Matthew 7:7-11, and in many other scriptures to seek him and you will find him. He wants us to seek him so he can put his Holy Spirit in us to guide us and give us his peace. I'm proof that he means what he says. I still make mistakes because I'm human, but he is always there for me and he will be there for you too. He loves all his children.

God speaks to us through the Bible. I've heard many people say the Bible is an old book. It's outdated, and it contradicts itself. Those people don't read and study it, or they're just not interested and make excuses. My answer to them is, "Look around you and see the beauty of nature on land, the skies, the universe, and under the sea. Any God that can create our magnificent universe, which works in split-second accuracy and in perfect order, can put a book in our world to guide us and tell us who he is. That book is the Bible. He speaks to us through his Word and his world. Don't miss out on God; your life depends on it.

Explanations and Some Interesting Bible Facts

The Bible is the only book and the most unique book ever written. It has forty-four authors and sixty-six books, and it was written over a period of more than 1,500 years. None of the authors was even a writer. They were regular people like you and I that God used to reach other people.

Like any other writings, you can take it out of context if you grab a line here or there to make it say what you want. The fact remains, from Genesis to Revelation, the message is the same. People are sinners, and God is loving, forgiving, and gracious. He loves the sinner but hates sin.

When the Bible has the word "fear," it does not always mean to be afraid. Many times it means to respect who God is. In translating, the word "fear" was used for respect in many places.

When you talk to God, read and study the Bible. Little by little, it comes together, and you start seeing a clearer picture. It's like a tapestry when woven together. The more you weave, the more beautiful and clearer it becomes.

Historically the Bible has shown to have accurate claims, even up until today. Everything started in the Middle East, and it is still happening today centuries later as the Bible predicts. It's all setting up for the return of Jesus. He came to our world as the Lamb, but he will return as the Lion of Judah. Jesus will come back at any moment, as he promised. Stay ready!

JANUARY 1

Believe and receive eternal life. Start the New Year with Jesus at your side. Make a fresh commitment to him.

Jesus said, "I am the way, the truth and the life. No one comes to the father but through me."

—John 14:6

JANUARY 2

God is our refuge. Never forget. He created you,
and he loves you. Trust Jesus in good times and
times of trouble. He will never leave you.

Trust in God at all times. Pour out your heart
before him. God is our refuge.

—Psalm 62:8

JANUARY 3

We have a duty to God, our Creator, and others. That
is to treat others as we want to be treated.

Fear God, and keep his commandments:
for this is the whole duty of man.

—Ecclesiastes 12:13

JANUARY 4

Never fear, for God is with you. The enemy of faith is fear. Over a hundred times in the Bible, God tells us to "fear not."

Fear not. I am with you, be not dismayed. I am your God. I will strengthen you, and help you.

—Isaiah 41:10

JANUARY 5

Discipline yourself, and always look to God in time of need. He alone can give you peace.

Discipline seems like a cause for grief, and not for joy, but later it brings forth the fruit of peace and justice to those who are trained in its school.

—Hebrews 12:11

JANUARY 6

Your choice now will set your future. Every choice
you make in life, you will have to live with.

Do not be deceived, God is not mocked; whatever
a man sows, this he will also reap.

—Galatians 6:7

JANUARY 7

Make no mistake in thinking God is not there. God is with us and watches us 24/7/365—every minute and every second.

Know that I am with you always.

—Matthew 28:20

JANUARY 8

Look to God for everything. Ask him to come into your heart and mind. Talk to him all the time, and he will guide you through life.

> For such is God, our God forever and ever;
> he will guide us until death.

—Psalm 48:14

JANUARY 9

The Ten Commandments were—and still are—the law of the universe. God knew we could never keep his commandments. They are guidelines for humankind. God gave his law to us through Moses, but he gave his love to us through Jesus.

For while the law was given through Moses, the enduring love came through Jesus Christ.

—John 1:17

JANUARY 10

Forgive and love one another. Forgiving means you may
remember the pain, but you still love the person.

Love one another, such as my love has been for
you, so must your love be for each other.

—John 13:34

JANUARY 11

Ask God to come into your life. Seek him with
all your heart, and you will find him.

Jesus tells us: ask, and you will receive, seek and you
will find. Knock, and it will be open to you.

—Matthew 7:7

JANUARY 12

Watch how you judge others because the same
judgment may come back to you.

If you want to avoid judgement. Stop passing judgement. The
verdict on others may be the verdict passed on you. The measure
with which you measure will be used to measure you.

—Matthew 7:1–2

JANUARY 13

Treat others the way you want to be treated.

Treat others the way you would have them treat you.

—Matthew 7:12

JANUARY 14

Happiness is when you thank God for everything. Laughter makes the heart happy. Make yourself laugh throughout the day, and you will find it soon comes naturally.

In everything give thanks, for this is the will of God.

—1 Thessalonians 5:18

JANUARY 15

Wisdom is a gift from God. Ask him for it.

Wisdom will multiply your days and add years to your life.

—Proverbs 9:11

JANUARY 16

Your values are the eyes of your soul.

Ill-gotten gain has no lasting value, but right living can save your life.

—Proverbs 10:2

JANUARY 17

Listen before you answer, and don't interrupt
anyone in the middle of his or her speech.

Everyone enjoys a fitting reply. It is wonderful
to say the right thing at the right time.

—Proverbs 15:23

JANUARY 18

Parents are contagious. Your children watch everything you
do and say. Be a good example because they will be who
you are. Cherish them. Show them love and affection. Use
wisdom, and be consistent in correcting their wrongs.

Children are a gift from God.

—Psalm 127:3

JANUARY 19

Always be honest with God. He knows everything anyway. There's nothing you can hide from him.

God knows the secrets of every heart.

—Psalm 44:21

JANUARY 20

Capture your ungodly thoughts before they capture you.

Your thoughts should be wholly directed to all that is true. Respectful, honest, pure, admirable, decent, virtuous or worthy of praise.

—Philippians 4:8

JANUARY 21

Worshipping God is not an event. It's a lifestyle.

Worthy are you, our Lord and our God, to receive glory
and honor and power; for you created all things.

—Revelation 4:11

JANUARY 22

When you face difficult times, you can use this formula:

1. Make sure your life is right with God.

2. Ask him for forgiveness for every sin.

3. Pray for God's wisdom and guidance.

He who obeys me [wisdom] dwells in security,
and in peace, without fear of harm.

—Proverbs 1:33

JANUARY 23

Don't just depend on what people tell you. Talk to God about everything. Give your life to Jesus, and read the Bible.

God our Father tells us: "I love those who love me, and those who diligently seek me will find me."

—Proverbs 8:17

JANUARY 24

If you live by the sword, you will die by the sword.

Jesus said, "Those who use the sword are
sooner or later destroyed by it".

—Matthew 26:52

JANUARY 25

Let anything you think or say be pleasing to God.

Let the words of my mouth and the thoughts
of my heart find favor before you.

—Psalm 19:14

JANUARY 26

Always pray for our nation and the people in office.

Blessed is the nation whose God is the Lord.

—Psalm 33:12

JANUARY 27

Never give into evil. Try hard always to do the right thing.

Turn from evil, and do good; seek peace, and follow after it.

—Psalm 34:14

JANUARY 28

It's normal to get angry. Just keep it under control.

The fool immediately shows his anger, but the shrewd (or) clever man passes over an insult.

—Proverbs 12:16

JANUARY 29

Never answer a person harshly.

A mild answer calms wrath, but a harsh word stirs up anger.

—Proverbs 15:1

JANUARY 30

Always speak positively. If you think negatively, don't say it.

Death and life are in the power of the tongue. Those
who make it a friend shall eat its fruits.

—Proverbs 18:21

JANUARY 31

Be careful what you speak.

He who guards his mouth and his tongue keeps himself from trouble.

—Proverbs 21:23

FEBRUARY 1

Don't tell your secrets to a fool; he or she will tell everyone.

Doing wrong is fun for a fool. While wise
conduct is a pleasure to the wise.

—Proverbs 10:23

FEBRUARY 2

God, from the beginning, gave you a free
will to choose your own destiny.

People who live only for wealth, come to the end of their lives
as naked and empty handed as the day they were born.

—Ecclesiastes 5:15

FEBRUARY 3

Life is not the absence of storms but how you get through them.

Jesus said, "Don't be afraid, take courage, I am here."

—Matthew 14:27

FEBRUARY 4

God's not asking us to understand, just to trust and have faith in him.

Commit your way to the Lord, and trust him.

—Psalm 37:5

FEBRUARY 5

Your family is a priceless treasure. Put them second only to God.

For where your treasure is, there your heart will be also.

—Matthew 6:21

FEBRUARY 6

Give your life to God, and stay close to him for protection
from evil. God created us, and he is our keeper.

The Lord will guard you from all evil. He will guard your life.

—Psalm 121:7

FEBRUARY 7

God said in his Word that you should obey and respect your parents.

Children, obey your parents in the Lord for
that is what is expected of you.

—Ephesians 6:1

FEBRUARY 8

There is more happiness in giving than receiving.

Recall the words of the Lord Jesus himself, who said,
there is more happiness in giving than receiving.

—Acts 20:35

FEBRUARY 9

I can do all things through Jesus.

If God is for us, who can be against us?

—Romans 8:31

FEBRUARY 10

Turn to God every day for his guidance. Confess your
sins to him even if you don't know what they are.

I sought the Lord, and he answered me and
delivered me from all my fears.

—Psalm 34:4

FEBRUARY 11

Watch what you say. What comes from
your lips can make or break you.

A man of knowledge uses words with restraint, and
a man of understanding is even-tempered.

—Proverbs 17:27

FEBRUARY 12

Turn away from any evil; it can destroy you before you realize it.

Detest what is evil, cling to what is good.

—Romans 12:9

FEBRUARY 13

Show love and respect for other people. Treat
them like brothers and sisters.

Be devoted to one another in brotherly love, give
preference to one another in honor.

—Romans 12:10

FEBRUARY 14

Love is action demonstrated.

Love is patient, kind, not jealous, not snobbish, never rude,
not self-seeking, hates wrong and loves truth, love endures.

—1 Corinthians 13:4–8

FEBRUARY 15

Choose carefully what you do in life; it always has consequences.

Happy is the man whose conscience does not
condemn what he has chosen to do.

—Romans 14:22

FEBRUARY 16

Hold on to what is good; avoid any evil.

Test everything, retain what is good, avoid any resemblance of evil.

—1 Thessalonians 5:21–22

FEBRUARY 17

Jesus said, "Learn of me and love me."

True love is from a pure heart. A good conscience and a sincere faith.

—1 Timothy 1:5

FEBRUARY 18

Money is not the root of evil. The love of money is the root of evil.

The love of money is the root of all sorts of evil. Some men in their passion for it, strayed from faith, and have come to grief and pain.

—1 Timothy 6:10

FEBRUARY 19

Flee from evil; seek what is good.

Flee from evil, instead, seek after Godliness, integrity, faith, love, steadfastness, and a gentle spirit.

—1 Timothy 6:11

FEBRUARY 20

Ask God to keep his spirit within you so you
can be strong, loving and wise.

God has not given us a spirit of timidity, but
of power and love and discipline.

—2 Timothy 1:7

FEBRUARY 21

Don't let emotions make your decisions.

Do you see a man who is hasty in his words? There
is more hope for a fool than for him.

—Proverbs 29:20

FEBRUARY 22

People change, but Jesus never does. He was not born; he is forever.

Jesus Christ is the same yesterday, today and forever.

—Hebrews 13:8

FEBRUARY 23

Seek happiness, not pleasures. Happiness gives us joy, but pleasures and self-indulgence lead to disappointment.

Happy is he who keeps the law.

—Proverbs 29:18

FEBRUARY 24

One way to keep healthy is by staying happy.
Trust God to keep you happy.

A joyful heart is health to your body, but a
depressed spirit dries up the bones.

—Proverbs 17:22

FEBRUARY 25

The ability to listen is the ability to learn.

Apply your heart to instructions, and your
ears to words of knowledge.

—Proverbs 23:12

FEBRUARY 26

You become what you expose yourself to.

Honor is the possession of wise men, but fools display dishonor!

—Proverbs 3:35

FEBRUARY 27

When you pray, you are talking to God. When
you read the Bible, God is talking to you.

Behold, I have written you on the palms of
my hands. You are ever before me.

—Isaiah 49:16

FEBRUARY 28

Love unites, and sin divides.

How good and pleasant it is when brothers live together in unity.

—Psalm 133:1

FEBRUARY 29

The best way to get even is to forgive and trust in God.

Say not, "I will repay evil." Trust in the Lord and he will help you.

—Proverbs 20:22

MARCH 1

Love is not self-getting, but self-giving. Consider
others more important than yourself.

You shall love your neighbor as yourself.

—James 2:8

MARCH 2

Look for Jesus in your life. He's waiting for you to respond to him.

For the one who asks, receives. The one who
seeks, finds. The one who knocks, enters.

—Matthew 7:8

MARCH 3

Don't let your pride keep you from listening to constructive criticism.

He who loves correction loves knowledge,
but he who hates reproof is stupid.

—Proverbs 12:1

MARCH 4

Love and respect can only happen if a husband and wife work at it together. It doesn't come easy. It does have to be earned. There should be no physical, mental, or verbal abuse in a marriage.

Wives respect your husbands; husbands, love and respect your wives.

—Ephesians 5:33

MARCH 5

What God wants from his children is gratitude, love, and praise because he gave us the gift of life and forgiveness through Jesus.

Give thanks to the Lord, for he is good, his kindness endures forever.

—Psalm 106:1

MARCH 6

Guard your lips; be careful what you speak.

Like gold or a wealth of jewels, wise lips are a precious thing.

—Proverbs 20:15

MARCH 7

There is nothing new under the sun. Everything has been said and done. The most important thing is how we handle life.

Solomon, the wisest, most wealthy man that ever lived said; what has been, that will be, what has been done, that will be done, nothing is new under the sun.

—Ecclesiastes 1:9–10

MARCH 8

Open your heart to God, and he will show you great
things beyond your reach of knowledge.

Thus says the Lord. Call to me, and I will answer you, and I will
tell you great and mighty things, which you do not know.

—Jeremiah 33:2–3

MARCH 9

Humility begins with self-examination.

Why look at the speck in your brother's eye
when you miss the plank in your own?

—Matthew 7:3

MARCH 10

Be careful how you judge others.

Your verdict on others will be the verdict passed on you.

—Matthew 7:2

MARCH 11

No one is perfect. We all make mistakes. Forgive everyone.

> If you forgive the faults of others, your heavenly
> Father will forgive you yours.

—Matthew 6:14

MARCH 12

When you feel overwhelmed with burdens in your life,
stop and share them with Jesus. He will help you.

Come to me, all, you who are weary and find
life burdensome, and I will refresh you.

—Matthew 11:28

MARCH 13

If you want pain in your life, pick the wrong people to be your friends.

Bad company corrupts good character.

—1 Corinthians 15:33

MARCH 14

The attitude you bring with you is the attitude you get from others.

Your attitude must be that of Jesus Christ.

—Philippians 2:5

MARCH 15

Be humble in your thoughts; overcome the idle of me.

Do nothing from selfishness or empty conceit.

—Philippians 2:3

MARCH 16

You live with the attitude you alone choose.

Keep alert and pray for an attitude of thanksgiving.

—Colossians 4:2

MARCH 17

If you are not at one with God, you won't be at one with each other.

He who upsets his household has empty air for a heritage.

—Proverbs 11:29

MARCH 18

Don't follow your heart. You were born with a sinful
heart. Follow your conscience. Take responsibility
for your own actions. Don't blame others.

Lord give me an understanding heart to
discern between right and wrong.

—1 Kings 3:9

MARCH 19

Look to God always. Read and keep his Word. His Word is life.

Pay attention to what I say. Listen carefully. Don't lose
sight of my words, let them penetrate deep in your heart
for they bring life to all who discover their meaning.

—Proverbs 4:20–22

MARCH 20

True success in life is when you laugh often, find the best in others, and give of yourself to others never being selfish.

Sharing your bread with the hungry, sheltering the oppressed, clothing the naked, and not turning your back on your own. Then God will guide you always, give you plenty, and he will renew your strength.

—Isaiah 58:7–11

MARCH 21

The joy you give others is the joy that comes back to you.

Trust in the Lord with all your heart, don't rely on
your own intelligence. In all your ways be mindful
of him, and he will make straight your path.

—Proverbs 3:5–6

MARCH 22

Jesus tells us to seek him. Read and study God's Word. There is a difference between honest doubt and doubt from lack of information. The scripture below is talking about unbelievers.

He says, being darkened in their understanding, excluded from the life of God because of the ignorance in them (lack of information); their hearts were hardened.

—Ephesians 4:18

MARCH 23

Sin will rob you of your love, joy, peace, and happiness.

Wisdom is of more value than foolishness,
    just as light is better than darkness.

—Ecclesiastes 2:13

MARCH 24

Sometimes failure is the first step to victory. Be
strong in the Lord and the power of his might.

God indeed is my savior, I am confident and unafraid,
my strength and my courage is in the Lord.

—Isaiah 12:2

MARCH 25

Spend fifteen minutes with God every day, and your life will change.

Trust in the Lord forever! For he is the eternal rock.

—Isaiah 26:4

MARCH 26

Life isn't fair. Don't expect it to be. We live in a fallen, sinful world.

Don't be afraid, for I am with you. Do not be dismayed, for I am your God. I will strengthen you and I will help you.

—Isaiah 41:10

MARCH 27

Jesus promised us to have clarity of mind, stability of
heart, and wisdom in speech if we seek him.

Seek the Lord while he may be found. Call on him while he is near.

—Isaiah 55:6

MARCH 28

Jesus, keep me safe every day and every night.

Keep me as the apple of your eye; hide me
in the shadow of your wings.

—Psalm 17:8

MARCH 29

If you are critical of others, it's probably because
you have more faults then they do.

Every one of you who pass judgment, you condemn
yourself; for you who judge practice the same things.

—Romans 2:1

MARCH 30

Be humble before God in all you do, and he will give you honor.

Humility goes before honor.

—Proverbs 15:33

MARCH 31

Love is extravagant. It is willing to pay the price. It is willing to give the time, it will endure hardship, and it is humble.

Jesus said, "A new commandment I give you, that you love one another, even as I have loved you."

—John 13:34

APRIL 1

Don't be a gossiper or a busybody. You will make a fool of yourself.

He who spreads accusations is a fool.

—Proverbs 10:18

APRIL 2

Listen to your conscience. It's a warning from God.

Blessed are they who maintain justice, who constantly do what is right.

—Psalm 106:3

APRIL 3

Focus on Jesus, and you will have lasting peace.

Present your needs to God in prayer and gratitude. God's own peace, which is beyond all understanding, will stand guard over your heart and mind in Jesus.

—Philippians 4:6–7

APRIL 4

Be free in Jesus, talk to him always, and listen to his Word.
God will keep you free from evil and worldly addictions.

Avoid evil, for evil people cannot sleep until they have caused
someone to stumble and did their evil for that day.

—Proverbs 4:16

APRIL 5

Be responsible for your actions.

Everyone should bear his own responsibility.

—Galatians 6:5

APRIL 6

Man's favorite strategy is to rationalize sin instead of repenting of it. Thank you, Father God, for your wisdom and insight. Help us to see things the way you see things.

May the God of our Lord Jesus Christ, the Father of glory, grant you a spirit of wisdom and insight to know him clearly.

—Ephesians 1:17

APRIL 7

God established marriage from the beginning, Adam and Eve, the first husband and wife. When you stand before God and say your marriage vows, God joins one man and one woman together.

God created man then he said, "I will make a helper for the man." God fashioned a woman [Eve] and gave her to Adam.

—Genesis 2:18–22

APRIL 8

Talk to God every day about everything,
just like you would a close friend.

Draw close to God, and he will draw close to you.

—James 4:8

APRIL 9

Father God, I ask in the name of Jesus, your Son, that you give me wisdom and faith. Help me to never doubt you and your Word.

Let him ask for wisdom and it will be given to him.
You must ask in faith. Never doubting.

—James 1:5–6

APRIL 10

Your tongue is like a spark that can set a huge forest
ablaze. A few words spoken in anger can destroy
a relationship that took years to build.

The tongue is a small thing, but what enormous damage it can do.

—James 3:5

APRIL 11

Be kind to each other, forgiving one another just as Jesus forgave you.

Be kind to one another compassionate, and forgiving
just as God has forgiven you in Christ Jesus.

—Ephesians 4:32

APRIL 12

God resists the arrogant, proud, and boastful,
but he bestows favor on the humble.

Clothe yourself with humility, because God is stern with
the arrogant; but to the humble, he shows kindness.

—1 Peter 5:5

APRIL 13

Sin is when you know you are doing wrong and continue to do it.

When a man knows the right thing to do and does not do it, he sins.

—James 4:17

APRIL 14

Sin will pass through your mind. But sin is not
sin until you dwell on it or act on it.

When lust has conceived, it gave birth to sin.

—James 1:15

APRIL 15

Believe in Jesus, and you will live forever.

You who believe in the name of the Son of God possess eternal life.

—1 John 5:13

APRIL 16

Honor your mom and dad, and God will bless you.

Honor your father and your mother, that you may have a long life in the land which the Lord your God is giving you.

—Exodus 20:12

APRIL 17

The Lord God Jesus is the alpha (first) and omega (last). He is, he was, and he is coming back again soon. Stay ready!

The Lord God says, "I am the alpha and omega, the one who is and who was and who is to come, the almighty."

—Revelation 1:8

APRIL 18

If Jesus is God in your life, he tells us over a hundred times in the Bible to "fear not" because he holds the keys to death.

There is nothing to fear. I am the first and the last, the one who lives. Once I was dead but now I live forever and ever. I hold the keys to death.

—Revelation 1:17–18

APRIL 19

Keep a close check on your thoughts. Every action
you take begins with a thought in your mind.

The start of strife is like the opening of a dam.
Therefore, check a quarrel before it begins.

—Proverbs 17:14

APRIL 20

Trust God to strengthen your heart with his love and his wisdom.

It is better to take refuge in the Lord than to trust in man.

—Psalm 118:8

APRIL 21

A positive person is a joyful person. He or she can make opportunities of his or her difficulties, but a negative person makes difficulties of his or her opportunities.

A joyful heart is good medicine.

—Proverbs 17:22

APRIL 22

Are you a perfectionist to a fault? Do you always think you're right? It must be hard for you to keep friends.

Fools think they need no advice, but the wise listen to others.

—Proverbs 12:15

APRIL 23

God loves a cheerful giver.

He who sows sparingly will also reap sparingly, and he
who sows bountifully will also reap bountifully.

—1 Corinthians 9:6

APRIL 24

The word "hope" is misunderstood. It's not always wishful thinking. I have hope because I can enjoy my earthly life knowing my future life is in heaven. Hope is a gift from God.

The hopes of the godly result in happiness.

—Proverbs 10:28

APRIL 25

Never tell a lie. It always comes back to you.

A lying tongue is only for a moment.

—Proverbs 12:19

APRIL 26

The greater the sin against you, the greater you have to pay to love and forgive. You can only do that if God is in your life.

Keep fervent (zealous-motivated) in your love for one another because love covers a multitude of sins.

—1 Peter 4:8

APRIL 27

Guard your thoughts! Pray every day for God's wisdom.
Use your time wisely, and keep away from evil.

The mind of a sinful man is death, but a mind
controlled by God's spirit is life and peace.

—Romans 8:6

APRIL 28

Pray these words every day, "Lord Jesus, draw me
close to you and teach me your ways."

Blessed are those who seek God with all their hearts.

—Psalm 119:2

APRIL 29

Be careful how you live, not as fools. Choose
your friends very carefully.

Don't be drunk with alcohol or drugs because that will ruin your life.

—Ephesians 5:18

APRIL 30

Are you a pessimistic person or a complainer? That's a sin! People don't like being around you. It brings you and them down. Ask Jesus every day to help your attitude.

God is our refuge and strength, a very present help in trouble.

—Psalm 46:1

MAY 1

Life is a gift from God. Unfortunately we take it for granted.

O Lord, since you are my rock and my fortress, for
the sake of your name, lead and guide me.

—Psalm 31:3

MAY 2

Finding God early in life is to find wisdom at an early age.

Knowing God leads to self-control, patience,
godliness, and love for others.

—2 Peter 1:6–7

MAY 3

Love and faithfulness go hand in hand.

Let love and faithfulness never leave you. Bind them
on the tablets of your heart. Then you will win favor
and a good name in the sight of God and man.

—Proverbs 3:3–4

MAY 4

Do you wear out people by smothering them?

Don't visit your neighbor too often or you will wear out your welcome.

—Proverbs 25:17

MAY 5

There is a name that is heavier than lead, "fool."

Stay away from fools, for you won't find knowledge there.

—Proverbs 14:7

MAY 6

A good listener is a wise man. He will learn much.

The wise are glad to be instructed, but
babbling fools fall flat on their faces.

—Proverbs 10:8

MAY 7

God's wisdom never fails. It was here before the world began.

Only fools despise wisdom and discipline.

—Proverbs 1:7

MAY 8

When a friend trusts you with a secret, never let him or her down.

It's better to say nothing than to promise something
that you don't follow through on.

—Ecclesiastes 5:5

MAY 9

Limit the time you spend with a fool. Tell him or her nothing. An ounce of foolishness can outweigh a pound of wisdom and honor.

A fool's mouth is his ruin.

—Proverbs 18:7

MAY 10

Are you arrogant? No one likes to be around an arrogant fool.

Pride leads to disgrace, but with humility comes wisdom.

—Proverbs 11:2

MAY 11

If God created the universe and our intricate bodies, he can certainly write his words through us that he created.

The Bible came from God through the men who wrote it. All scripture is inspired by God.

—1 Timothy 3:16

MAY 12

Money is not the root of all evil; the love
of money is the root of all evil.

Those who love money will never have enough.

—Ecclesiastes 5:10

MAY 13

If you think God is not answering your prayers, it's because
the answer is no, wait or your motive was wrong.

You ask God and do not receive because you ask with wrong motives.

—James 4:3

MAY 14

Are you a gossip? If you're not part of the problem
or solution, then you're gossiping.

As sure as a wind from the north brings rain,
so a gossiping tongue causes anger.

—Proverbs 25:23

MAY 15

Can you keep a secret? No one likes or trusts a
big mouth. They are usually deceitful.

The one who desires life, to love and see good days, must keep
his tongue from evil and his lips from speaking deceit.

—1 Peter 3:10

MAY 16

Before making a decision, stop and ask God for wisdom.

God tells us, "I set before you, life and prosperity, and death and adversity."

—Deuteronomy 30:15

MAY 17

Thank God every day for the healing of your body,
mind, and soul, whether you are sick or not.

God is faithful.

—1 Corinthians 1:9

MAY 18

God made each person special. Be different. Be yourself.

God created man in his image; male and female he created them.

—Genesis 1:27

MAY 19

Your mind is the control tower of your life.

Thou wilt keep him in perfect peace, whose mind is stayed on God.

—Isaiah 26:3

MAY 20

God promised his followers, clarity of mind,
stability of heart, and wisdom in speech.

For I will give you the right words and wisdom.

—Luke 21:15

MAY 21

Only when you see life as God sees life can you be content.

Are you not aware that you are the temple of God,
and that the spirit of God dwells in you?

—1 Corinthians 3:16

MAY 22

You are only an attitude away from success.

Never let evil talk pass your lips, say only the good things
men need to hear, things that will really help them.

—Ephesians 4:29

MAY 23

How do you respond to sin? Your sin affects everyone around you. Be more aware of the consequence.

Keep a good conscience. It's better that you suffer for doing what is right, rather than for doing what is wrong.

—1 Peter 3:16–17

MAY 24

It is possible to give without loving, but it is
impossible to love without giving.

Give your service willingly; do it for God, rather than men.

—Ephesians 6:7

MAY 25

Disobedience leads to anguish and human
suffering, the inevitable result of sin.

He who walks honestly walks securely, but he
whose ways are crooked will fare badly.

—Proverbs 10:9

MAY 26

Faith is not a feeling. It's a choice. Faith operates in a spiritual realm.

It's through faith that a righteous person has life.

—Romans 1:17

MAY 27

Expect more from yourself and less from others.

Love your enemies, do good to those who hate you.

—Luke 6:27

MAY 28

Negative thoughts and conversation will bring
you and the people around you down.

Pleasing words are a honeycomb sweet to
the taste and health to the body.

—Proverbs 16:24

MAY 29

Respect or disrespect in a man or woman is earned.

A wise man is cautious and turns away from
evil, but a fool is arrogant and careless.

—Proverbs 14:16

MAY 30

Where will you spend eternity? Life is short, but eternity is forever.

God tells us to seek good, not evil, that you may live eternally.

—Amos 5:14

MAY 31

God owns everything. We are only managers
of what he gives to us here on earth.

Do not layup treasures on earth that can rust, corrode
and be stolen. But store up heavenly treasures that
will not rust or corrode. They are eternal.

—Matthew 6:19–20

JUNE 1

Remember, you can only be respected if you earn it.

A good name is better than good ointment.

—Ecclesiastes 7:1

JUNE 2

When you hold a grudge toward someone, you become a slave to him or her. When someone hurts you, give it to God and free yourself because God tells us in his Word.

He is your strength in time of trouble. He will help you.

—Psalm 37:39–40

JUNE 3

Finding fault with others is like washing windows.
All the dirt is on the other side.

Lord, cleanse me from my unknown faults.

—Psalm 19:12–13

JUNE 4

Fear drives out faith.

God tells us to "fear not," for I have redeemed you;
I have called you by name, you are mine.

—Isaiah 43:1

JUNE 5

It's right to do right, even when it's right to do wrong.

Truly the evil man shall not go unpunished,
   but those who are just shall escape.

—Proverbs 11:21

JUNE 6

Do you have trouble admitting you are wrong? Usually
it's due to pride, insecurity, and inadequacy.

The wise look ahead to see what is coming,
but fools deceive themselves.

—Proverbs 14:8

JUNE 7

Our decisions in this life have eternal consequences.

The way of the fool seems right in his own eyes,
but he who listens to advice is wise.

—Proverbs 12:15

JUNE 8

Bible wisdom is our defense against temptation.

Say to wisdom, "you are my sister." Call understanding, "your friend."

—Proverbs 7:4

JUNE 9

If you are not at one with God, you won't be at one with each other.

The Lord protects the upright, but destroys the wicked.

—Proverbs 10:29

JUNE 10

Always be positive and uplifting to others.

He who refreshes others will himself be refreshed.

—Proverbs 11:25

JUNE 11

Evil talk leads to evil thoughts; evil thoughts lead to evil actions.

Walk with wise men and you will become wise,
but a companion of fools shall fare badly.

—Proverbs 13:20

JUNE 12

Every time we turn green with envy, we are ripe for trouble.

A tranquil [calm] mind gives life to the
body, but jealousy rots the bones.

—Proverbs 14:30

JUNE 13

It's better to build strong children than to have to repair adults.

Train a child in the way he should go, and when
he is old he will not depart from it.

—Proverbs 22:6

JUNE 14

Humility is not thinking little of yourself; it's not thinking of yourself.

Do not think of yourself more highly than you ought, but rather think of yourself with sober judgment, in accordance with the measure of faith God has given you.

—Romans 12:3

JUNE 15

When one's temper gets the best of him or her,
it reveals the very worst of him or her.

A quick-tempered man does foolish things.

—Proverbs 14:17

JUNE 16

Learn how to speak kind words, and no one will resent you for them.

Let your conversation be always full of grace and seasoned with salt.

—Colossians 4:6

JUNE 17

You can't change the past, but you can ruin the
present by worrying over the future.

Cast all your cares on God because he cares for you.

—1 Peter 5:7

JUNE 18

Love is a circle without end, never narrow and always bending.

If I have faith that can move mountains,
but have not love, I am nothing.

—1 Corinthians 13:2

JUNE 19

A child of God is not one that never falls, but is
one that gets up and goes on every time.

Let us not grow weary of doing good. If we do not relax
our efforts, in due time we shall reap our harvest.

—Galatians 6:9

JUNE 20

Lord Jesus, help me to remember the things I should not forget and forget the things I should not remember.

Love your enemies and pray for those who persecute you.

—Matthew 5:44

JUNE 21

There are 86,400 seconds in a day. Just take a few
to talk to God. He has given you so many.

This is the day the Lord has made; let us rejoice and be glad in it.

—Psalm 118:24

JUNE 22

Anger makes your mouth work faster than your mind.

A fool gives full vent to his anger, but a wise
man keeps himself under control.

—Proverbs 29:11

JUNE 23

Some people dress better, and other people eat better, but those people who look to God have peace and sleep better.

Better a little with virtue than a large income with injustice.

—Proverbs 16:8

JUNE 24

Talk to Jesus every day. Ask him to make
you strong in your belief in him.

The world's sin is unbelief in Jesus.

—John 16:9

JUNE 25

God gave us life to enjoy, not to abuse.

I (Jesus) have come that they may have life, and have it to the full.

—John 10:10

JUNE 26

Walk and talk to Jesus every chance you get,
and you will be like Psalm 1:3.

You will be like a tree planted near running water whose
leaves never fade. (What you do will prosper).

—Psalm 1:3

JUNE 27

Don't take for granted today what you could lose tomorrow.

Show me, o Lord your way, and lead me on a level path.

—Psalm 27:11

JUNE 28

Life is a victory to those who believe in Jesus.

The Lord is my strength and my shield.

—Psalm 28:7

JUNE 29

Put your faith and trust in Jesus. He will always be there for you.

My trust is in you, o Lord, you are my God.

—Psalm 31:14–15

JUNE 30

Happiness is having Jesus in your life.

Taste and see how good the Lord is; happy is
the man who takes refuge in him.

—Psalm 34:8

JULY 1

Turn away from anger and wrath or getting even. It will
only harm you. The price of vengeance is high.

Never avenge yourself, leave it to God for it is written. "I will take
vengeance; I will repay those who deserve it," says the Lord.

—Romans 12:19

JULY 2

The way God measures faith is by what your faith will endure.

The Lord loves what is right and will never leave his faithful ones.

—Psalm 37:28

JULY 3

God created us to love him so he could live through
us and we would learn to love him.

Create in me a clean heart, O God, and renew your spirit within me.

—Psalm 51:10

JULY 4

God bless our great country. Help each and every
one of us to say as in Psalm 56:3–4.

In God I trust without fear.

—Psalm 56:3–4

JULY 5

The secret of victorious living is to face God before you face man.

The Lord is my light and my salvation; whom should I fear?

—Psalm 27:1

JULY 6

Humble does not mean to degrade yourself. It
means to put yourself last and others first.

God is opposed to the proud, but gives grace to the humble.

—James 4:6

JULY 7

Read a scripture a day. When the term "hearing and hearing" is used, it means to meditate on God's work. As you live your life before God, you will learn faith.

Faith comes by hearing and hearing the Word of God.

—Romans 10:17

JULY 8

If someone told you that Jesus would be with you
today, how would you act? "Because he is."

Teach me Lord your way that I may walk
in your truth, direct my heart.

—Psalm 86:11

JULY 9

The key to an easier life is to make wise decisions in your youth. "Keep God's commandments."

Those who keep God's commandments
remain in him and he in them.

—1 John 3:24

JULY 10

The word "success" before the word "work" is only found in the dictionary. There is no success without work.

People who work hard sleep well.

—Ecclesiastes 5:12

JULY 11

Are you selfish? Live as though everyone is
more important than you are.

For wherever there is jealousy and selfish ambition,
there you will find disorder and every kind of evil.

—James 3:16

JULY 12

The Ten Commandments are a necessity to guide you through life successfully. God tells us how important they are in his Word.

Drill them into your children, speak of them at home, bind them at your wrist, and write them on the doorpost of your house.

—Deuteronomy 6:7–8

JULY 13

Put God first before anything. He is your guide. Always put your guide up front because he knows the way.

You shalt have no other gods before me.

—First Commandment Exodus 20: 3

JULY 14

We dishonor God when we use his name to swear.

Thou shalt not take the name of the Lord, thy God, in vain.

—Second Commandment Exodus 20:7

JULY 15

God gave us seven days in a week. He asked
if we would share one with him.

Remember the Sabbath day to keep it holy.

—Third Commandment Exodus 20:8

JULY 16

God wants us always to honor and respect our parents,
just as Jesus did when he lived on earth.

Thou shalt honor thy father and thy mother.

—Fourth Commandment Exodus 20:12

JULY 17

God said in his Word, "If you live by the
sword, you will die by the sword."

Thou shalt not kill.

—Fifth Commandment Exodus 20:13

JULY 18

When you marry and promise yourself to one person, you should never let yourself get intimately involved with someone else.

Thou shalt not commit adultery.

—Sixth Commandment Exodus 20:14

JULY 19

If it doesn't belong to you, it isn't yours. Then you have no right to it.

Thou shalt not steal.

—Seventh Commandment Exodus 20:15

JULY 20

If you don't have anything good to say about someone, don't say anything. Above all, never lie about another person.

Thou shalt not bear false witness against thy neighbor.

—Eighth Commandment Exodus 20:16

JULY 21

Ask God to keep you satisfied with what you have
and not be jealous or envious of others.

Thou shalt not covet [desire] thy neighbor's house.

—Ninth Commandment Exodus 20:17

JULY 22

Live within your means. Ask God to help you never
desire or dwell on what another person has.

Thou shalt not covet [desire] thy neighbor's wife nor his
manservant, nor anything that is thy neighbors.

—Tenth Commandment Exodus 20:17

JULY 23

The greatest commandment God gave us is in Matthew 22:37–38.

Jesus said, "You shall love the Lord your God with all
your heart, all your soul, and with all your mind; and
you should love your neighbor as yourself."

—Matthew 22:37–38

JULY 24

This is an old proverb, "I hear, and I forget; I see and don't remember; I do, and I understand."

Jesus says, "Follow me."

—Matthew 4:19

JULY 25

Don't dwell on people that did you wrong. God sees
all things. He will handle your enemies.

God tells us, "Vengeance is mine, I will repay."

—Hebrews 10:30

JULY 26

Draw close to Jesus, and he will increase your faith.

Who then is the conqueror of the world? The one
who believes that Jesus is the Son of God.

—1 John 5:5

JULY 27

Patience, gentleness, meekness, and humility
are strength under control.

Everyone must be quick to hear, slow to speak and slow to anger.

—James 1:19

JULY 28

Earth is our classroom, but heaven is our home. God's
commandments were not intended to save people,
but to point out sin so we can correct it.

For the commandments are a lamp, and the teaching
is light. They correct and discipline our lives.

—Proverbs 6:23

JULY 29

Are you an insensitive person?

Singing cheerful songs to a person whose heart is heavy is as bad as stealing someone's jacket in cold weather, or rubbing salt in a wound.

—Proverbs 25:20

JULY 30

God is breathtaking! He is everywhere, always watching.

God will judge the secrets of men through Christ Jesus.

—Romans 2:16

JULY 31

Are you a liar? The truth will keep you at
peace, but a lie will eat at you.

Our Lord hates a lying tongue.

—Proverbs 6:16–17

AUGUST 1

Don't always follow the desires of your
heart. They can lead you astray!

We can gather our thoughts. But the Lord gives us the right answers.

—Proverbs 16:1

AUGUST 2

Immorality is a sin against God and your own body.

Flee immorality.

—1 Corinthians 6:18

AUGUST 3

When you have a problem, don't look at the problem.
Look to Jesus. He is always there to help you.

Bow humbly under God's mighty hand, so that
in due time he may lift you high.

—1 Peter 5:6

AUGUST 4

Am I a bad listener?

He who gives an answer before he hears, it is folly and shame to him.

—Proverbs 18:13

AUGUST 5

God created knowledge. If you need more, ask
him. He will give you what you need.

My thoughts are not your thoughts, nor are your ways my ways, says
the Lord. As high as the heavens are above the earth, so high are
my ways above your ways and my thoughts above your thoughts.

—Isaiah 55:8–9

AUGUST 6

When God closes a door, he opens another one. Don't keep looking at the door he closed. You will miss out. Move on!

God, the holy one, who opens and no one can close, who closes and no one can open.

—Revelation 3:7

AUGUST 7

Believe and receive eternal life. Believe in Jesus and live forever.

For God so loved the world that he gave his only Son (Jesus),
that whoever believes in Jesus will have eternal life.

—John 3:16

AUGUST 8

God said to read and study his words.

Search the scriptures.

—John 5:39

AUGUST 9

God asks that we live a clean and wholesome
life with the life he gave us.

If you live according to my teaching, than you will
know the truth and the truth will set you free.

—John 8:31–32

AUGUST 10

Don't look to another person for your happiness.
Happiness is within yourself.

Lord, in your presence is fullness of joy.

—Psalm 16:11

AUGUST 11

People who set goals for their lives have a greater sense of direction. They are excited about life and have remarkable energy. They are creative and usually very healthy.

He who plans things will be successful.
Happy, is he who trusts in the Lord.

—Proverbs 16:20

AUGUST 12

Setting goals is the key to success on earth and in heaven.

Hard work means prosperity; only fools waste away their time.

—Proverbs 12:11

AUGUST 13

God desires your success.

Keep this book [the Bible] of the law on your lips. Recite
it by day and by night so you know what is written in
it than you will successfully attain your goal.

—Joshua 1:8

AUGUST 14

Success includes having the right attitude.

Be firm, be steadfast, do not fear, for the Lord
your God is with you everywhere you go.

—Joshua 1:9

AUGUST 15

You are never alone, as God tells us in Joshua 1:5.

I will not leave you nor forsake you.

—Joshua 1:5

AUGUST 16

One of the greatest deceptions comes when we think success is wealth.

> Trust in the Lord and do good, that you may
> dwell in the land and enjoy security.

—Psalm 37:3

AUGUST 17

Are you rude?

A fool does not delight in understanding, but
only in revealing his own mind.

—Proverbs 18:2

AUGUST 18

Dependence on God is a principle ingredient to success.

For I know the plans I have for you, plans for welfare
and not calamity to give you a future and hope.

—Jeremiah 29:11

AUGUST 19

There are three things in making a good sound decision:

1. Get the facts before you answer.

2. Be open to new ideas.

3. Make sure you hear both sides of a story
    before you answer or judge.

Intelligent people are always open to new ideas.

—Proverbs 18:15

Any story sounds true until someone sets the record straight.

—Proverbs 18:17

AUGUST 20

Are you sarcastic? Sarcasm hurts! Avoid sarcasm. It makes enemies.

Patience can persuade a prince, and a soft
speech can crush strong opposition.

—Proverbs 25:15

AUGUST 21

Are you argumentative?

Avoiding a fight is a mark of honor, only fools insist on quarreling.

—Proverbs 20:3

AUGUST 22

When you cheat, you are cheating yourself!

A good name is to be more desired than great wealth.

—Proverbs 22:1

AUGUST 23

Through God's wisdom, man can do anything, but
the mind of a fool destroys what he touches.

Happy is the person who finds wisdom and gains understanding.

—Proverbs 3:13

AUGUST 24

Gossip is wrong! If it's about someone else
today, it will be about you tomorrow.

Do not associate with a gossip.

—Proverbs 20:19

AUGUST 25

Be wise in innocence and unwise in evil.

God grants a treasure of good sense to the godly. He is
their shield, protecting those who walk with integrity.

—Proverbs 2:7

AUGUST 26

Am I a loner?

He who separates himself seeks his own desire.
He quarrels against all sound wisdom.

—Proverbs 18:1

AUGUST 27

What you say can lift up someone or tear them down.

The words of a man's mouth are deep waters.

—Proverbs 18:4

AUGUST 28

Discipline your child often, but show him or her love
more often. Spend quality time with your children.

If you refuse to discipline your children, it proves you don't love them.

—Proverbs 13:24

AUGUST 29

God gives us a free will, but his desire is that we come to him.

I am the door. If anyone enters through me, he will be saved.

—John 10:9

AUGUST 30

Do you hurt people with your words?

Some people make cutting remarks. But the
words of the wise bring healing.

—Proverbs 12:18

AUGUST 31

The name Jesus means life to us. We are his sheep.

Jesus said, "My sheep hear my voice and I know them and they follow me; I give them eternal life and they shall never perish."

—John 10:27–28

SEPTEMBER 1

God still does miracles today. He is the same God. He never changes. The God of the Old Testament is the same God as his Son Jesus in the New Testament. He told us in Isaiah 49:15–16.

> I will never forget you. Upon the palms of my
> hands I have written your name.

—Isaiah 49:15–16

SEPTEMBER 2

Never compare yourself to anyone. God made you unique in
yourself. You are the only person like you that God made.

God told his son Jesus. Let us make man
in our image, after our likeness.

—Genesis 1:26

SEPTEMBER 3

God stands at the door of our hearts and
knocks for us to invite him in.

God said, "I am the searcher of hearts and minds."

—Revelation 2:23

SEPTEMBER 4

Strive to keep your conscience clear before God and man.

Paul said, I do my best to always maintain a
blameless conscience before God and man.

—Acts 24:16

SEPTEMBER 5

God tells all children to obey their parents.

You children, obey your parents in everything.

—Colossians 3:20

SEPTEMBER 6

Always seek what is good. Turn your back on evil.

He who pursues evil will have evil befall him.

—Proverbs 11:27

SEPTEMBER 7

Wisdom in life is to endure what you must and change what you can.

My son be wise, and guide your heart in the right way.

—Proverbs 23:19

SEPTEMBER 8

Jesus is a humble king that left his perfect kingdom to come to an imperfect and sinful world to save us all from evil. He loved and served people when he was here, and we should do the same.

Jesus picked up a towel, poured water in a basin and began to wash his disciple's feet and dry them with the towel.

—John 13:4–5

SEPTEMBER 9

Don't be a boastful fake! An old country preacher once
said, "If you ain't what you is, you is what you ain't."

Like clouds and wind when no rain follows is the man
who boastfully promises what he never gives.

—Proverbs 25:14

SEPTEMBER 10

Weigh what you say.

Like golden apples in silver settings are
words spoken at the proper time.

—Proverbs 25:11

SEPTEMBER 11

The key to success is setting goals. To find the goals God
has given you, you have to spend time with him.

Your heavenly Father knows all your needs. Seek first his kingship
and his holiness, and all other things will be given to you.

—Matthew 6:32–33

SEPTEMBER 12

Are you a jealous person? Jealousy is insecurity and greed.

Jesus said, "Beware! Don't be greedy for what you don't have."

—Luke 12:15

SEPTEMBER 13

Many times charm and beauty are deceptive, but a good woman brings good and not evil all the days of her life.

When one finds a worthy wife, her value is far beyond pearls.

—Proverbs 31:10

SEPTEMBER 14

Are you lazy? Today is the day; tomorrow is procrastination.

An idle man will suffer hunger.

—Proverbs 19:15

SEPTEMBER 15

Meekness is not weakness. It's strength
under control and brings peace.

He [Jesus] was in the form of God. He emptied
himself and took the form of a slave.

—Philippians 2:6–7

SEPTEMBER 16

An important lesson in life is to learn to value the things that really matter: God, family, your work, and friends.

Enjoy what you have rather than desiring what you don't have. Dreaming about it is meaningless.

—Ecclesiastes 6:9

SEPTEMBER 17

Heaven and earth can pass away, but God's Word will stand forever.

Blest are they who hear the Word of God and keep it.

—Luke 11:28

SEPTEMBER 18

A good attitude will bring you success; a bad one will bring failure.

In everything you do, act without grumbling or arguing.

—Philippians 2:14

SEPTEMBER 19

Don't put off today what you still will have to do tomorrow.

Make the most of every opportunity.

—Colossians 4:5

SEPTEMBER 20

Greed will make you a lonely person, but sharing makes good friends.

The fate of everyone greedy: unlawful gain takes
away the life of him who acquires it.

—Proverbs 1:19

SEPTEMBER 21

Some people ask, "If God is loving, how can he send people to hell?"
He doesn't! People send themselves to hell. Remember, he gives us free
will and a conscience to discern right from wrong. It's our choice.

Our God is patient, wanting none to perish but
that all would repent and come to him.

—2 Peter 3:9

SEPTEMBER 22

Discuss problems with maturity; avoid an argument.

Bear with one another; forgive whatever grievances you have
against one another, forgive as God has forgiven you.

—Colossians 3:13

SEPTEMBER 23

Continually practice virtue [good morals].

You are a chosen child of God. Clothe yourself with
mercy, kindness, humility, meekness and patience.

—Colossians 3:12

SEPTEMBER 24

Respect one another, and in return, others will respect you.

Let your speech be always gracious and in good taste,
strive to respond properly to all who address you.

—Colossians 4:6

SEPTEMBER 25

God puts love in our heart for other people.
We should practice it more often.

God said for us to love one another as I have loved you.

—John 15:12

SEPTEMBER 26

Seek God's wisdom, and patience will follow.

A man's wisdom gives him patience; it is to
his glory to overlook an offense.

—Proverbs 19:11

SEPTEMBER 27

God gave us his Ten Commandments and
the Bible to guide us through life.

Lord your word is a lamp to my feet and a light to my path.

—Psalm 119:105

SEPTEMBER 28

Having to be right is a life of unending conflict.

Get rid of all bitterness, wrath and anger, harsh
words, slander, and malice [harm to others].

—Ephesians 4:31

SEPTEMBER 29

Go to Jesus. Be honest before him. Never make excuses for yourself. He knows all things and can help you.

My child, listen to me and treasure my instructions.

—Proverbs 2:1

SEPTEMBER 30

Spiritual experience leads to spiritual knowledge of God.

My people perish for lack of knowledge.

—Hosea 4:6

OCTOBER 1

Are you critical of others?

The wise are known for their understanding and instruction is appreciated if it is well presented.

—Proverbs 16:21

OCTOBER 2

"Be not afraid." Never forget. God tells us in
his Word that he will never leave us.

God said, "I will never desert you, nor will I forsake you."

—Hebrews 13:5

OCTOBER 3

Parents, correct and guide your children, but don't provoke them. Love and praise them. Spend time with them, but raise them to be responsible adults.

Fathers, do not provoke your children to anger, but bring them up in the discipline and instruction of the Lord.

—Ephesians 6:4

OCTOBER 4

Don't lie because it causes people to doubt everything you say.

Wise men store up knowledge, but with the
mouth of the foolish, ruin is at hand.

—Proverbs 10:14

OCTOBER 5

Love and respect your spouse. Keep your marriage pure by keeping your intimate moments between just you and your spouse.

Marriage is to be held in honor among all.

—Hebrews 13:4

OCTOBER 6

Are you two-faced?

Blessings are on the head of the righteous, but the
mouth of the wicked conceals violence.

—Proverbs 10:6

OCTOBER 7

It's important what you confess. Confess defeat, and you will be defeated. Confess victory, and you will be victorious.

By your words you will be acquitted, and by your words you will be condemned.

—Matthew 12:37

OCTOBER 8

Don't pick on others because you're having a bad day.

Quarrel not with a man without cause, with
one who has done you no harm.

—Proverbs 3:30

OCTOBER 9

Lord Jesus, I confess all my sins to you: the ones I know and the ones I don't know or remember.

The king [God] takes delight in honest lips.

—Proverbs 16:13

OCTOBER 10

Once truth is broken, confidence no longer exists.

He who utters lies is a betrayer.

—Proverbs 14:25

OCTOBER 11

When your life is not right and everything seems to be wrong, Jesus says, "Turn to me. I will straighten out your life. Trust in me."

Jesus said, "Come to me all who are weary and find life burdensome, and I will refresh you."

—Matthew 11:28

OCTOBER 12

If you don't have anything nice to say, just don't say anything.

A soothing tongue is a tree of life, but a perverse one crushes the spirit.

—Proverbs 15:4

OCTOBER 13

God bless America and heal our land.

Virtue [good morals] exalts a nation, but sin is a people's disgrace.

—Proverbs 14:34

OCTOBER 14

Stay away from depression. Keep your life simple and light.

Every day is miserable for the depressed, but the lighthearted man has a continual feast.

—Proverbs 15:15

OCTOBER 15

The key to happiness is to give yourself away.

He who is generous will be blessed, for he gives to the poor.

—Proverbs 22:9

OCTOBER 16

Good sense is a vital part of people. It can make or break you.

My children, listen to me, pay attention, and grow wise.

—Proverbs 4:1

OCTOBER 17

You can know a person by the company he or she keeps.

Declare a tree good and its fruit is good; declare a tree rotten
and its fruit is rotten. You can tell a tree by its fruit.

—Matthew 12:33

OCTOBER 18

Do not lower your standards to accommodate others.

A single reprimand does more for a man of
intelligence than a hundred lashes for a fool.

—Proverbs 17:10

OCTOBER 19

Surround yourself with those who tell the truth,
not necessarily what you want to hear.

Some friends bring ruin on us, but a true
friend is more loyal than a brother.

—Proverbs 18:24

OCTOBER 20

A fool's mouth is his ruin, but humility goes before honor.

It is not what goes into a man's mouth that makes
him impure, it's what comes out of his mouth.

—Matthew 15:11

OCTOBER 21

Haste makes waste!

He who acts hastily, blunders.

—Proverbs 19:2

OCTOBER 22

Turn your cheek. God said to forgive seventy times seven.

Peter asks Jesus, "How often must I forgive him, 7 times?"
Jesus replied, "No, not 7 times, but 70 times 7."

—Matthew 18:21–22

OCTOBER 23

Laziness brings about poverty.

Love not sleep, lest you be reduced to poverty.

—Proverbs 20:13

OCTOBER 24

Jesus loves the pure of heart.

He who pursues justice and kindness will find life and honor.

—Proverbs 21:21

OCTOBER 25

Pray for faith. Faith is being sure of what we hope
for and certain of what we do not see.

Anyone who comes to God must believe that he exists,
and that he rewards those who seek him.

—Hebrews 11:6

OCTOBER 26

Do you make fun of people?

He who mocks the poor taunts his maker. He who
rejoices at calamity will not go unpunished.

—Proverbs 17:5

OCTOBER 27

If you give your life to God, he can guide and protect you. But
if you don't, he can't always protect you. [It's your choice.]

God said, "My son, give me your heart, and
let your eyes keep to my ways."

—Proverbs 23:26

OCTOBER 28

Your wisdom in God will last forever, but
body muscle deteriorates with age.

A wise man is more powerful than a strong man.

—Proverbs 24:5

OCTOBER 29

If you feel good about someone else's problems,
ask God to help you. You need it.

Rejoice not when your enemy falls, lest the Lord
see it and be displeased with you.

—Proverbs 24:17–18

OCTOBER 30

Wrong thinking is, "Whatever wrong you did me, I will do you."

God tells us, say not, "as he did to me, so will I do to him,"
I [God] will repay the man according to his deeds.

—Proverbs 24:29

OCTOBER 31

When you lie to others, you will eventually lie to yourself.

A lying tongue is its owner's enemy.

—Proverbs 26:28

NOVEMBER 1

A cheerful heart is medicine to your bones.

Guard your heart for it is the source of life.

—Proverbs 4:23

NOVEMBER 2

Most of the time, your problem is right under your nose [your mouth].

> Words from the wise man's mouth win favor,
>   but the fool's lips consume him.

—Ecclesiastes 10:12

NOVEMBER 3

God lives within you. Keep your heart, mind, and body clean.

God says, "My home is within you."

—1 Corinthians 3:16

NOVEMBER 4

When you have Jesus in your life, you have wisdom, peace, strength, love, hope, truth, success, forgiveness, faith, happiness, and security.

Call to intelligence and understanding, seek her[(wisdom]
like a hidden treasure than you will understand the fear
of the Lord; the knowledge of God you will find.

—Proverbs 22:3–5

NOVEMBER 5

Your tongue is a messenger from the heart.

Like choice silver is the just man's tongue; the
heart of the wicked is of little worth.

—Proverbs 10:20

NOVEMBER 6

Your words make a difference.

Evil words destroy one's friends; wise discernment rescues the godly.

—Proverbs 11:9

NOVEMBER 7

Anger resides in the bosom of fools. We need to forgive others for ourselves. If we don't forgive, we will become bitter.

Do not associate with a hot-tempered man, lest you learn his ways.

—Psalm 22:24–25

NOVEMBER 8

It is much easier to live with the truth than suffer with
a lie. The world lies to us, and we lie to ourselves.

God has counsel instore for the upright, he will shield
those who walk honestly, wisdom will enter your
heart and knowledge will please your soul.

—Proverbs 2:7, 10

NOVEMBER 9

The Lord turns his back on the house of the
wicked, but blesses the house of the just.

My son, forget not my teachings, many days and
years of life and peace they will bring you.

—Proverbs 3:1–2

NOVEMBER 10

Cursing is a sign of ignorance.

Let no unwholesome word proceed from your mouth, but only words good for edification.

—Ephesians 4:29

NOVEMBER 11

Don't take yourself so seriously. Some
mistakes can be turned into humor.

A glad heart lights up the face, but mental anguish breaks the spirit.

—Proverbs 15:13

NOVEMBER 12

Your thoughts become your words. Your words become your actions. Your actions become your character. Your character becomes your destiny.

He who finds me [God's wisdom] finds life and favor from the Lord.

—Proverbs 8:35

NOVEMBER 13

Blessings come from obedience to God.

When a man walks in integrity and justice,
happy are his children after him.

—Proverbs 20:7

NOVEMBER 14

A wise man gains knowledge when instructed,
but a fool is arrogant and turns his back.

The wise man is cautious and shuns evil.

—Proverbs 14:16

NOVEMBER 15

The love of parents to a child softens the rules of their household.

He who loves his child takes care to chastise [correct] him.

—Proverbs 13:24

NOVEMBER 16

Children brought up by parents in a loving, disciplined, and caring home will make stable, loving, and caring parents to their children.

The rod of correction gives wisdom, but a boy left
to do as he wants disgraces his mother.

—Proverbs 29:15

NOVEMBER 17

The pride of boasting about yourself is a sign of insecurity and a sin.

Jesus said, if you boast in your arrogance, such boasting is evil.

—James 4:16

NOVEMBER 18

Integrity has nothing to do with wealth, knowledge, or position.

Better a poor man who walks in his integrity than
he who is crooked in his ways and rich.

—Proverbs 19:1

NOVEMBER 19

A fool despises your godly wisdom. Don't waste it on him or her.

Speak not for the fools hearing. He will despise your godly wisdom.

—Proverbs 23:9

NOVEMBER 20

Ignorance of scripture is ignorance of God.

Scripture, the source of wisdom.

—2 Timothy 3:15

NOVEMBER 21

Anxiety and worry can destroy your peace and wear you down.

Jesus said, which of you by worrying can
add a moment to his life span?

—Matthew 6:27

NOVEMBER 22

The way you think today determines the
quality of life you have tomorrow.

Teach me to do your will, for you are my God.

—Psalm 143:10

NOVEMBER 23

The more you trust God, the more you find him faithful.

Jesus told his disciples, "For man it is impossible;
but for God all things are possible."

—Matthew 19:26

NOVEMBER 24

Thanksgiving is a time for us to thank God for who he
is and all he has done for us. However, it would be for
our benefit to take time every day to thank him.

Give thanks to the Lord for he is good. His kindness endures forever.

—1 Chronicles 16:34

NOVEMBER 25

The Bible is knowledge waiting to be learned.

Paul prayed that we may learn to value the things that really matter.

—Philippians 1:10

NOVEMBER 26

Jesus Christ, Alpha and Omega

God said, "The name of Jesus is above every other name."

—Philippians 2:9

NOVEMBER 27

All that you have today and all that you are today is a
result of what you believed and said yesterday.

In all your ways acknowledge him and he shall direct your paths.

—Proverbs 2:6

NOVEMBER 28

Don't worry! It's pointless! It brings on stress, anxiety, and depression. Half the time, it doesn't happen, and the other half of the time, it can't be avoided.

Do not worry.

Matthew 6:31

NOVEMBER 29

Keep close to God so you are not deceived
and you can discern good from evil.

The Lord will strengthen you and guard you against evil.

—2 Thessalonians 3:3

NOVEMBER 30

When you suffer for a wrong that was done to you, you
have a choice of resentment or hope and joy.

Do not return evil for evil, or insult for insult. The one who desires
life and to see good days must turn away from evil and do good.

—1 Peter 3:9–11

DECEMBER 1

Jesus is the shepherd. We are his sheep.
Celebrate Jesus's birth this month.

Jesus said, "I am the good shepherd. For
these sheep, I will give my life."

—John 10:14–15

DECEMBER 2

Pray these words, Father. Forgive me in the name of your Son
Jesus for every sin I ever committed. Thank you for saving
me from evil. Come into my life. Put in me your wisdom.
And for all eternity, I want to be with you. Amen.

God did not send his son into the world to condemn us,
but that the world might be saved through him.

—John 3:17

DECEMBER 3

Invest your time wisely in this life God has
given you. It has eternal consequences.

A short span you have made my days. Only
a breath is any human existence.

—Psalm 39:5

DECEMBER 4

Talk to Jesus about everything. Trust in
him, and he will build your faith.

Do not let your hearts be troubled. Have faith in God.

—John 14:1

DECEMBER 5

Genuine forgiveness of others will benefit ourselves a
hundred times more than the person we forgive.

A kind man benefits himself.

—Proverbs 11:17

DECEMBER 6

Jesus is the light. Walk with him, and you will never be in darkness.

Jesus said, "I am the light of the world. He who possesses the light [Jesus] has life."

—John 8:12

DECEMBER 7

Jesus came so we could have a purpose for living. So be happy, smile, and turn to Jesus for everything.

Jesus said, "I am the resurrection and the life; whoever believes in me, though he should die, will come to life."

—John 11:25–26

DECEMBER 8

Do you want to be free? Worry about nothing,
and pray about everything.

God indeed is my savior; I am confident and unafraid.
My strength and my courage is the Lord's.

—Isaiah 12:2

DECEMBER 9

Jesus Christ is the visible image of the invisible God,
God the Father. He once died for sin for all.

The fool says in his heart, "There is no God."

—Psalm 14:1

DECEMBER 10

God our creator put together one man and one woman
for marriage, not any other combination. Who are we
to change what he declared from the beginning?

A man leaves his father and mother and clings to his wife, and
the two of them become one body. God blessed them saying;
be fertile and multiply; fill the earth and subdue [control] it.

—Genesis 2:24

DECEMBER 11

Children, respect your parents. God put them in charge to teach you obedience and love.

The Lord set a father in honor over his children; a mother's authority he confirms over her sons and daughters. Honor your father and mother.

—Ephesians 6:2

DECEMBER 12

If you don't have anything positive to say, keep your mouth shut.

A talebearer separates bosom friends.

—Proverbs 16:28

DECEMBER 13

Run from evil. It will destroy you. Whatever you
choose to obey becomes your master.

Do not let sin control you. Ask Jesus to be the master of your life.

—Romans 6:16

DECEMBER 14

A man who has a habit of abusive language
will never mature in character.

Like a city that is broken into and without walls is
a man who has no control over his spirit.

—Proverbs 25:28

DECEMBER 15

Do you give your opinion before people ask for it?
Wise people don't make a show of their knowledge,
but fools broadcast their lack of good sense.

A prudent man conceals knowledge, but the
heart of a fool proclaims folly.

—Proverbs 12:23

DECEMBER 16

Are you selfish? You can't find peace when you live to please yourself.

Each of us should look to others' interest rather than to our own.

—Philippians 2:4

DECEMBER 17

Trust in God rather than man. God knows
more about you than you do.

They who trust in the Lord are like Mount Zion,
immovable and will stand forever.

—Psalm 125:1

DECEMBER 18

Don't be negative! It takes too many muscles to frown. Be positive! You use very few muscles and look wonderful.

For the Lord will be your confidence.

—Proverbs 3:26

DECEMBER 19

Don't look back. It will disorient you. Always look forward. It keeps you sharp and alert.

Everyone begotten of God conquers the world.

—1 John 5:4

DECEMBER 20

Do you show your temper to often?

A man of great anger will bear the penalty, for if you
rescue him, you will only have to do it again.

—Proverbs 19:19

DECEMBER 21

Don't act like you know it all. You will most
likely make a fool of yourself.

Keep sound wisdom and discretion.

—Proverbs 3:21

DECEMBER 22

Christmas is about salvation, that is, God keeping his promise by sending his Son Jesus.

Blessed be the Lord God of Israel. Because he has visited and ransomed his people as he promised through the prophets of ancient times.

—Luke 1:68, 70

DECEMBER 23

Try to comprehend the love Jesus has for us. He left his holy place to come live among us to be treated like a criminal. It's worse than a king leaving his palace to live among street people that hate him. He lowered himself because he loves us and wants to help us.

Jesus said for us to love one another.

—John 15:17

DECEMBER 24

That baby in the manger so sweet and small
was God in the flesh to save us all.

The word became flesh and dwelt among us.

—John 1:14

DECEMBER 25

The ultimate Christmas gift of love is God giving us his Son Jesus.

Jesus said to God the Father, as you Father, are in me, and
I in you, I pray that they [people] may be one in us.

—John 17:21

DECEMBER 26

God has a plan for your life. Seek God about your
success. However, success from a human perspective
is often different than success God's way.

Keep careful watch over your conduct, don't act like a fool,
and make the most of the present opportunities.

—Ephesians 5:15

DECEMBER 27

God did his part in reaching out to you through Jesus. Now you have to do your part and reach back to him. It's your choice.

When anyone acknowledges that Jesus is the Son of God, God dwells in him and he in God.

—1 John 4:15

DECEMBER 28

Accept guidance and don't regel while you are young. Rebellion only leads to poor choices that can mess up your life.

For lack of guidance, people fall.

—Proverbs 11:14

DECEMBER 29

A stubborn man is a self-centered man that wants his way at any cost.

Just as it is not good to eat too much honey, it is not good
for people to think about all the honors they deserve.

—Proverbs 25:27

DECEMBER 30

Be careful what friends you trust. You may only have a couple friends in your lifetime that are true loyal friends.

A friend is always loyal.

—Proverbs 17:17

DECEMBER 31

End the year with God and your loved ones [family], and start the New Year with them. Only God and the people that love you will stick by your side through anything.

Help carry one another's burdens.

—Galatians 6:2

PRAYER

Thank you, Father God, for another year added to my eternal life you gave me through Jesus. Help me to be the person you designed me to be. Thank you for never leaving my side and always working to guide and direct me to your truths. Draw me closer to you and open my eyes to clearly see my need for you. Help me to love you and others the way you love me. Amen. Praise your holy name forever!

Jesus is still the only celebrity in the universe.

Quoted by my pastor Bil Gebhardt

CONCLUSION

It's more important what God says than what our culture speaks. Don't think like a fool. Don't take your future for granted. Be wise and trust God with your life. Remember, we are living in a fallen and sinful world, but God is always in control, and we sometimes don't understand. He permits what he hates to achieve what he loves.

Proverbs 3:13 says, "Blessed is the man who finds wisdom and gains understanding." Malachi 3:6 reads, "I the Lord, do not change." Revelation 1:8 states, "'I am the alpha [first] and the omega [last],' says the Lord God, 'who is, who was and who is to come, the almighty.'"

REFERENCES

The abbreviated scriptures I used in the calendar are from the New American Standard Bible [NASB] and the Ryrie NASB Study Bible.

There are pastors and teachers who can help you along the way as you read the Bible. They have messages online and books you can read. I list a few here: Billy Graham, John McArthur, Chuck Swindoll, David Jeremiah, John Piper, Howard Hendricks, Charles Spurgeon, and my pastor and teacher Bil Gebhardt. There are others, but these are the ones I know and trust. Their teachings line up with the Bible and Jesus's life as he walked our earth teaching God's Word.

Printed in the United States
By Bookmasters